MUMMIES

THE NEWEST, COOLEST & CREEPIEST
FROM AROUND THE WORLD

SHELLEY TANAKA

Archaeological Consultation by PAUL BAHN

SCHOLASTIC INC.

New York   Toronto   London   Auckland   Sydney
Mexico City   New Delhi   Hong Kong   Buenos Aires

A Scholastic / Madison Press Book

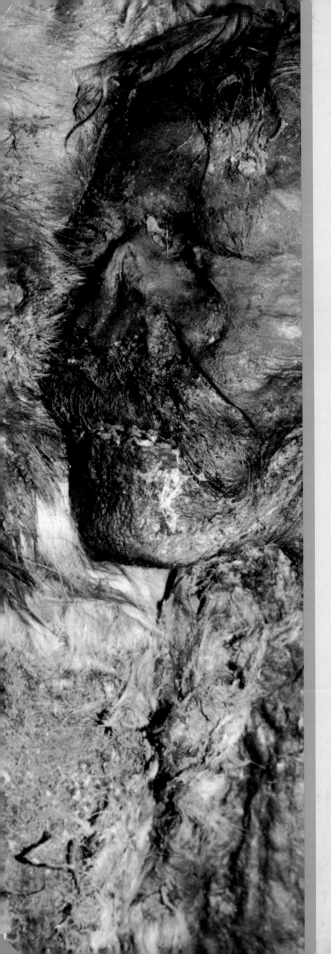

Mummies...

Right away we think of the ancient Egyptians, who embalmed and dried dead bodies, wrapped them in cloth bandages, and buried them in secret underground tombs. But a mummy can be any body whose soft tissues — skin, muscles, organs — have been preserved after death. Sometimes this is done deliberately, by humans. Sometimes mummies are made accidentally, by natural processes such as freezing or drying.

Every living thing decays when it dies. Dead plants rot and crumble. Dead animals, including insects, fish, birds, and humans, also rot. First the softest, most watery tissues decay — the eyes and internal organs. Then the flesh falls apart and crumbles. Finally, only teeth and bones remain, but they, too, will rot over time. The organic material that was once a living thing is returned to the soil, so more plants and animals can grow. It is nature's way of recycling.

In a mummy, the natural process of decay is stopped. It takes a great deal of human effort, or an unusual condition of nature, to make this happen. Preserving a dead body for thousands, even hundreds, of years is extremely difficult. That's why mummies are so rare and why it is so remarkable when we find them.

Yet we do find them — lying under ancient houses, hidden in desert sands, tucked away in remote mountain caves, trapped in thick layers of ice. As the planet gets warmer and icy areas begin to melt, as our roads and cities spread out and grow, we are discovering more mummies than ever before.

Where are these mummies? What do they look like? What are we doing with them, and what are they telling us?

(Opposite) A thousand-year-old mummy from Siberia. (Clockwise from top left) A burial mask from the Bahariya Oasis in Egypt; the colorful coffin of a mummy from the Saqqara Pyramids south of Cairo; the slumbering face of Cherchen Man; an ancient bust of Tutankhamun; a Chinese woman who died 1,700 years ago.

The fact that the New World has old mummies may seem surprising. Yet mummies have been discovered in many parts of the Americas, including the southwestern United States. Native Alaskans once wrapped their dead in bird skins, animal furs, and grass mats, and left them to dry in caves heated by underground volcanoes. And the Atacama Desert in Chile, one of the driest places on the planet, was once used as a burial ground by people who were making mummies even before the ancient Egyptians.

Some of the most recent mummy finds are coming to light as a result of global warming. We now know that as the world's glaciers continue to melt, they will leave behind garbage, weapons, clothing — and bodies — that have been frozen and preserved over thousands of years. Some of these finds will be archaeological treasures, telling

THE AMERICAS

scientists how ancient people used plants and tools, and traded with their neighbors.

Archaeologists do not have much time to find these defrosted mummies. Once the bodies are exposed, nature will continue the job of decay. Vultures, rodents, insects, and bacteria will consume any organic matter, and then the information mummies hold will be lost forever.

In some parts of South America, mummy researchers are racing against other pressures. Sometimes developers are anxious to build new roads or houses on top of an ancient cemetery. And sometimes the threat comes from thieves. Armed with axes and dynamite, they rummage through tombs looking for jewelry and statues, often tossing away the most scientifically valuable finds — the mummies themselves.

The mummy of the Cotton King was unearthed from a schoolyard in Tupac Amaru, Peru. His nickname comes from the three hundred pounds of cotton in which he was wrapped. He holds a piece of fabric, a shell, and a ball of chalky lime. Researchers are carefully cleaning and sketching the mummy and his possessions.

The World's Oldest Mummy Makers

Seven thousand years ago, even before the Egyptians made their first mummies, the Chinchorro people of South America were carefully preserving their dead. The Chinchorro lived in small villages tucked between the Pacific Ocean and the desert. They spent their days fishing in the sea, harvesting seaweed and grasses, and hunting deer and wild llama in the river valleys. They also mummified their dead — old and young alike.

Some bodies were just wrapped up tightly and left to dry in the hot Atacama Desert. Others were more carefully prepared. Like the ancient Egyptians, the Chinchorro knew that the key to preserving a body was removing the soft tissues that would decay most easily. So they took the body apart limb by limb and stripped off the skin and flesh. They also removed the internal organs and cut the skull in half to remove the brain.

(Above) This mummy was found on a stick mat used by the Chinchorro to carry babies. Its head is encased in mud. (Right) A child mummy is supported by a long stick that pokes through the top of its head.

The Chinchorro are named after an area in the Atacama Desert, near Arica, Chile.

Arica •

Mt. Llullaillaco

Then the body had to be put back together. The bones were reinforced with sticks, and the body cavities were packed with feathers, ashes, clay, fur, and reeds. The body was covered with a paste made of white ash and the skin was replaced, sometimes using sea lion or pelican skins to fill any gaps. Finally, the mummy was painted black, and perhaps given a clay mask and wig.

It was a lot of work. Perhaps too much. Several thousand years later (2500 to 2000 BCE), the Chinchorro mummies were prepared in a simpler way. The muscles and internal organs were removed through cuts in the torso and shoulders. The cavities were stuffed and sewn shut with a cactus spine needle threaded with human hair. Then the bodies were covered with ash paste and painted red. Some faces were repainted several times, suggesting that the mummies may have been put on display for a while, sometimes propped up with a stick, before being buried in the family graves.

The oldest manmade mummy ever found (from 5050 BCE) belongs to a Chinchorro child. Perhaps children and babies were the first to be mummified by their grieving mothers. And there must have been a lot of grief in those villages. Almost a quarter of the mummies found at one location in northern Chile were children who had died before they were a year old.

This thousand-year-old mummy, found by a fisherman who sat it upright, was preserved naturally by the dry desert climate. He or she died long after the Chinchorro stopped mummifying their dead. Instead, the body was simply buried along the coast, as were countless others.

Gifts for the Gods

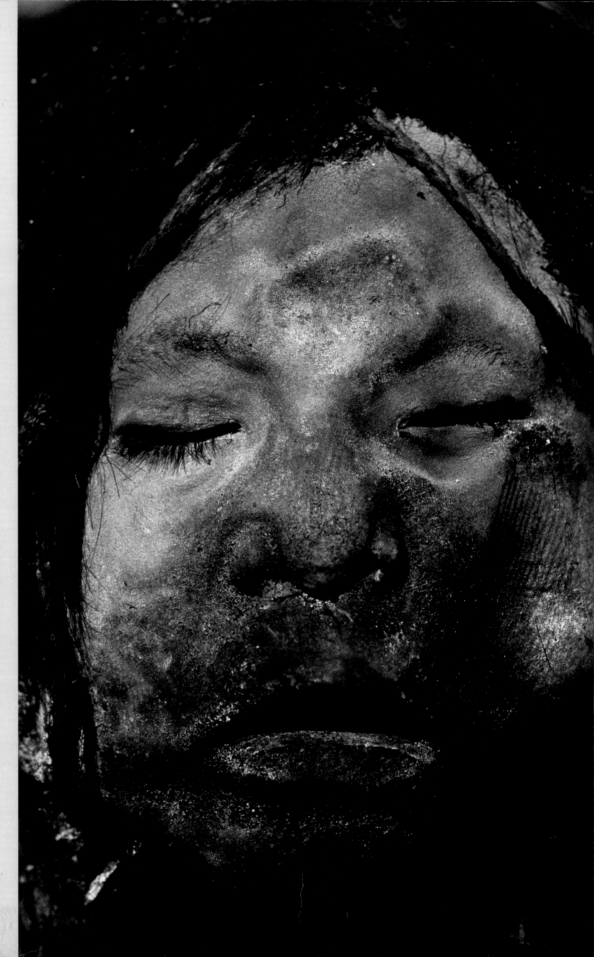

In 1999, in small stone-lined tombs at the top of Mount Llullaillaco, one of the highest mountains in South America, archaeologists found the frozen mummies of three Inca children — two girls and a boy — aged eight to fourteen. The girls' hair had been painstakingly braided, and the fourteen-year-old girl had been buried with a magnificent white feathered headdress. Along with the mummies were more than thirty small statues made of gold, silver, and shells, bundles of woven cloth, moccasins, and pots of food.

The children's faces were calm. They looked as if they were sleeping. Yet historians think they were left on the mountain as human sacrifices five hundred years ago.

Before the arrival of the Spanish invaders, the Inca ruled over twelve million people in a vast empire that stretched from Colombia to Chile. They were master artists and builders who constructed magnificent walled cities tucked into the steep slopes of the Andes. Life on the cold, windswept mountains was difficult. Drought, hail, or blizzards could wipe out a village's food supply. To make sure they had good harvests and healthy livestock, the Inca took gifts up the mountain and left them for the gods.

The gifts had to be very special. Not just their best statues, feathers, shells, and cloth but something even more precious — their children.

The children were dressed in the finest clothes and led up the mountain in a solemn procession. Some were strangled or clubbed on the back of the head before being bundled and placed in a tomb with other offerings. Only the most beautiful and healthy children were sacrificed, and it was considered a great honor to be chosen.

The Inca did not write, but their mummies can tell historians what these people ate, what they wore, how they died, and even who their relatives were. The Llullaillaco mummies were in such good condition that frozen blood still filled their hearts and lungs. (Most mummies have no fluids left in their bodies for scientists to study.) Their blood can be analyzed to see what diseases they had. DNA tests showed that the two girls found on Mount Llullaillaco were related. Comparison with modern DNA samples has even turned up a descendant of one of the girls living in Washington, D.C.

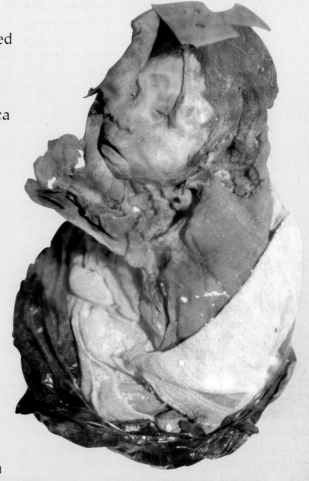

Aside from the burn marks, the younger girl's body was in good condition.

The mummy of the eight-year-old girl (opposite) still smelled of charred flesh when it was found on top of Mount Llullaillaco. A lightning strike sometime after her death left burn marks on her left ear, shoulder, and chest.

The older girl's mummy was buried with a fabulous white feathered headdress similar to the ones on these Inca statues (right).

Buried Beneath the Living

An Inca stone relief.

Dozens of Inca mummies were discovered in 2004 on a barren hillside on the outskirts of Lima, Peru, one of South America's largest cities. Archaeologists also uncovered grave goods and tools belonging to textile makers, who crafted the finely woven and feathered bags, blankets, and shawls, for which the Inca were famous.

However, researchers had little time to admire their find. The hill was standing right in the path of a new highway, and bulldozers were waiting to move in.

The discovery turned out to be part of an enormous Inca cemetery spread out over several acres of land. Many mummies had already been rescued from graves lying below a nearby shantytown. Although the bodies had remained perfectly preserved for hundreds of years in the dry desert, waste water from the settlement had seeped into the ground, causing many of the mummies there to decompose. The entire cemetery, called Puruchuco, may contain as many as 10,000 bodies and 60,000 grave objects, including food, beads, utensils, feathers, jewelry, pottery, and textiles — all buried for the dead to use in the afterlife.

Digging up these mummies has not been easy. The bodies were wrapped in bundles, some containing as many as seven individuals, some buried in family groups. One bundle was so heavy it took four men to lift it. Inside was the body of a man researchers called the Cotton King. He had been wrapped in three hundred pounds of raw cotton, which had to be picked away tuft by tuft to make sure no grave goods were tangled up in it.

Archaeologists will be studying the find for many years. The graves include the rich (buried with basic necessities as well as colorful bird feathers, weapons, seashells, and fine clothing) and the not-so-rich

(buried just with everyday items like pottery and food). The cemetery contained the bodies of adults, children, and babies. Examining the mummies will give scientists new information about the health of the Inca people, how they were related to each other, what they ate, how they died, and how they were able to establish a mighty and far-reaching empire that lasted only a few hundred years, until it fell to Spanish invaders in the 1500s.

Bundles of Mummies

The Inca often wrapped their dead in bundles, called *fardo*, before burial. The bodies were folded in a tucked position, then wrapped in cloth along with food and various possessions. Some bundles contained colorful cloaks and elaborate feathered headdresses. Feathers were prized by many native people, who traveled long distances to collect them.

Some bundles were even given wigs and fake heads — cloth stuffed with cotton — to make them look more human. The bundles may have been propped up and displayed before being buried.

More than half of the mummies in the Puruchuco cemetery are children. In ancient South American civilizations, children often died young. Many had anemia, likely caused by parasites — tiny intestinal worms that eat a person's blood.

The Cotton King's bundle (top) included sweet potatoes, corn, a warrior's club, and a headband that might have been used as a slingshot. There was also a baby in the bundle. (Right) An X ray of a different bundle shows a number of items, including a spondylus shell (circled). These shells — symbols of wealth — were only found far away in the waters off Ecuador.

Frozen Mummies

There hunters found the torso of a man sticking out of the ice at the edge of a glacier in northwestern Canada in 1999. The body had been torn apart by the shifting glacier, and the head and right arm were missing.

Tests of the native man's clothing, including a robe made from the pelts of ninety-five gophers, showed that he lived about 550 years ago, decades before Christopher Columbus arrived in the New World. When his body was discovered, native people from the area named him Kwaday Dan Ts'inchi, meaning "long ago person found." No photos of his body were allowed to be published. He was in his late teens or early twenties and healthy. Yet, while making a long trek through the mountains,

Tatshenshini-Alsek Park

perhaps to trade with people on the other side, he had somehow frozen to death before being covered by snow.

When the native elders heard about the frozen mummy, they were not in the least surprised. Their legends are full of tales of people who left home one day to cross the glaciers — and never returned.

(Background) Kwaday Dan Ts'inchi lay at the edge of this glacier in British Columbia. Four years later, two of the same hunters discovered his head not far away. Who knows what else may be uncovered as the world's glaciers and ice sheets continue to retreat?

(Opposite) Among the possessions with Kwaday Dan Ts'inchi's body were a long wooden spear, some dried salmon, and a sacred medicine pouch, which was not opened. A sheath (middle) was found with a knife handle (right). The handle had a rust-colored stain at one end, suggesting it had once held an iron blade. Before the arrival of the Europeans, native people had no metal tools. The iron was probably salvaged from a shipwrecked boat that had drifted ashore from Asia. There was also a wide-brimmed hat (left) made from the roots of a spruce tree. The hat had been woven tightly, making it waterproof.

Can Ancient Mummies Carry Disease?

The viruses locked away in frozen mummies may still be contagious when the bodies are thawed. Researchers are very careful when they work with these mummies. Heat and moisture from the researchers' own lungs may reactivate ancient bacteria or viruses that are not familiar to their modern immune systems.

Occasionally, scientists actually go searching for a sick mummy.

The Spanish Flu swept the globe in 1918, killing as many as forty million people before it ran its course and disappeared. Experts say it is only a matter of time before another deadly flu hits, and they want to be prepared to fight it.

Scientists have attempted to find the live virus in the bodies of several Spanish Flu victims who were buried in frozen ground. Most have been too decayed to provide good samples. Recently, however, four bodies were dug up in a cemetery in Brevig Mission, Alaska. One of them, a woman, contained fragments of the virus. The woman's frozen lung tissue was full of blood with the virus still in it after eighty years. The body was unusually well preserved because the woman was obese. In certain wet, cool conditions, the fat layer in the body can turn into a waxy, soaplike, acidic substance called adipocere. The acids help stop decay and can even preserve the internal organs by shielding them from the outside environment.

Scientists may now be able to figure out why the Spanish Flu was so dangerous, and perhaps even create a vaccine to stop another deadly flu epidemic.

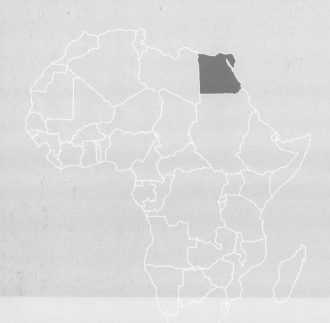

Preserving bodies was an important part of the ancient Egyptians' religion. They believed that a person's spirit lived on after death. During the day the spirit would leave the tomb, but at night it would return. If the dead did not look lifelike, the spirit would not recognize its body.

The mummies were made in many different ways, but the basic goals remained the same: stop decay and make the body look as lifelike as possible. The soft tissues like the brain and stomach were removed, and the body was carefully dried using natron salt. Then the body was washed with milk and wine, rubbed with perfume and stuffed with linen, mud, or reeds. Finally, it was decorated with jewelry and sacred amulets, wrapped in cloth, and perhaps covered with a lifelike mask of the dead person before being placed in a coffin and buried in a tomb.

EGYPT

(Above) The tomb of Tutankhamun contained many treasures, including this scarab. (Opposite) Tutankhamun's outermost coffin was made of gilded wood.

The body was to stay in the tomb, undisturbed, for eternity.

But the mummies were not left in peace. For thousands of years, grave robbers have ransacked tombs looking for valuables, simply tossing the mummies aside as garbage. Many Egyptian mummies were sold to museums and to tourists. Others were even burned as fuel or ground up and used as medicine.

Today, new mummies are still coming to light — including both the oldest manmade Egyptian mummy yet found and the very first lion mummy. And in 1996, a donkey made a spectacular discovery when it stumbled into a hole in Bahariya, near Cairo. The opening was part of a two-thousand-year-old cemetery containing as many as ten thousand mummies.

Royal Homecoming

• Cairo

• Bahariya Oasis

Valley of • the Kings

What happens to mummies once they have been found, dug up, and stripped of their valuables? Where do they go? Who owns them?

Not long ago, a royal mummy finally returned home after spending 150 years traveling abroad. Like many Egyptian treasures, the mummy had been stolen from a tomb and sold to a foreigner. It ended up in a small museum in Niagara Falls, Canada, where it was displayed alongside a two-headed calf, stuffed tigers, shrunken heads, and the barrels of daredevils who had gone over the Falls.

The mummy was eventually sold to a university in Atlanta, Georgia, where it was studied closely. Radiocarbon dating, X rays of the skull, an examination of the fine resin and linen used to fill the skull and chest, and the position of the arms indicated the mummy was royal. It may well be the long-lost pharaoh Ramses I, the grandfather of Ramses the Great.

Egypt has long been calling for a return of mummies that were taken out of the country illegally, and in 2003, the Atlanta mummy was given back. The flag-draped coffin was carried through the streets of Cairo in a horse-drawn carriage to its new home in the Egyptian Museum.

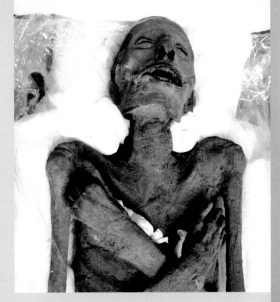

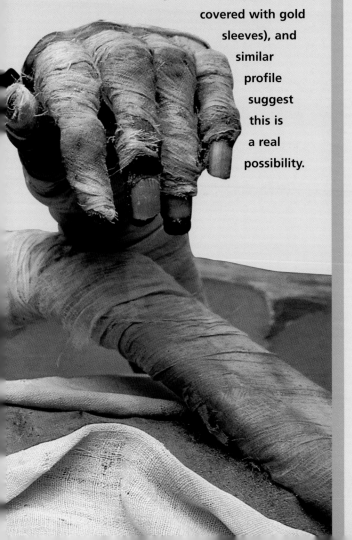

Is the Atlanta mummy (above) the grandfather of Ramses the Great (below)? The crossed arms (a position reserved for kings), splayed toes (which may once have been covered with gold sleeves), and similar profile suggest this is a real possibility.

A Very Modern Egyptian Mummy

Researchers recently made a real mummy (below) using the same tools, oils, spices, and techniques as the ancient Egyptians. The body belonged to a man who had donated his remains to science. The modern mummifiers removed the brain by sticking a hooked instrument up the nose and whisking it around to liquefy the tissue. "The brain tissue poured out pink, with a little blood, like a strawberry milkshake," said one of the researchers. They extracted the internal organs by reaching up through a small cut in the abdomen, just as the Egyptians did. "Imagine sticking your hand inside a dark, crowded closet and untangling the clothes.... You have to feel your way through."

Then the body was covered with 580 pounds of natron salt and left to dry until it was half its original weight. Finally, the mummy was rubbed with oils, wrapped in cloth, and placed in a casket. From time to time it will be checked for signs of decay, to see whether modern embalmers can match the skill of the Egyptian masters.

What Happened to Tutankhamun?

The mummy of the Egyptian pharaoh Tutankhamun was discovered by Howard Carter in a tomb filled with dazzling treasures in 1922. The body lay inside three coffins, the innermost one made of solid gold.

The open coffin was placed under the hot desert sun to melt the resins so the mummy's priceless gold mask could be removed. The bandages were chiseled away with hot knives, and the pharaoh's limbs, torso, and head were cut apart to release the 143 bracelets, daggers, and amulets that covered the body. Then, when there were no valuables left, the naked mummy was returned to its tomb in pieces and left to crumble.

It was only many years later that people became interested in the mummy itself. Why did the young pharaoh, who would have been given the best of everything, die when he was only nineteen years old? There were many theories. X rays led some experts to believe he had died from a blow to the head. Others noticed damaged vertebrae, suggesting he may have had a deformed spine that left him unsteady on his feet. Still others were sure that missing ribs meant his chest had been crushed. Was Tutankhamun murdered? Or did he have a tragic accident?

In 2005, scientists set out to answer the questions once and for all. The mummy was removed from its tomb and placed in a CT scanner (a three-dimensional X-ray machine). An examination of more than 1,700 images showed there was no evidence of murder. The damage to the skull, spine, and chest was likely caused by the embalmers and

(Above) Howard Carter, second from left, watches as Tutankhamun's wrappings are cut. (Below) A 2005 reconstruction shows what the young pharaoh may have looked like in life.

archaeologists who handled the body (right). Scientists did discover that the pharaoh's left leg was broken, but could not agree on when or how the break occurred. Had the leg wound become infected, eventually causing death? Or had the break been caused after death?

We will probably never know. Even with all the tools of modern science at our disposal, some things, it seems, will remain a mystery.

The Valley of the Kings contains the tombs of pharaohs such as Tutankhamun and Ramses the Great.

The Mummy's Curse

After the tomb of Tutankhamun was discovered, newspapers around the world reported that the find was cursed. They claimed there was an inscription on the tomb warning that "Death shall come on swift wings to him who disturbs the peace of the king." As if to prove the matter, Carter's pet canary was said to have been swallowed by a cobra at the very moment the tomb was discovered.

The story of the curse has been popular ever since. No one, it seems, wants to give it up. Now they may have to. In 2002, an Australian researcher traced the fates of all twenty-five Westerners who were present when the tomb and coffins were opened. There was no curse, he reported. Those present at the opening lived to an average age of seventy.

In this painting from a wall of Tutankhamun's tomb, the pharaoh (right) is embraced by the god Osiris (left) as he enters the underworld.

19

You may not expect to see many new mummies in Europe, a continent that has been settled and built up for thousands of years. But mummies have been found here, too. Several unusual items have been discovered behind the walls of houses in Great Britain, including letters, seashells, shoes — and mummified cats. Historians believe superstitious homeowners often placed dead cats behind the walls of homes to frighten evil spirits, and perhaps scare away mice and rats. Over hundreds of years, the cats were dried out and were preserved in the wall cavities, suddenly turning up — to the surprise of the homes' renovators!

Some of the strangest European mummies emerge from a peculiar landscape called the peat bog — stagnant, waterlogged lowlands with unusual preserving abilities. Several bog mummies have been found

EUROPE

This three-hundred-year-old mummified cat was found in the wall of a house in Edinburgh, Scotland.

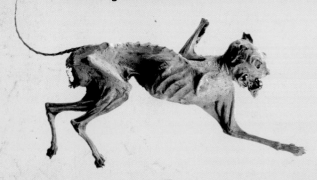

dating back to the Iron Age two thousand years ago, including Grauballe Man (opposite), whose naked body was found by peat-diggers in Denmark in 1952. His throat had been slit from ear to ear, and his right arm was twisted behind his back. His skin was so well preserved that researchers were able to take his fingerprints, yet the bog had dissolved all of his tooth enamel.

In 2001, new technology, including a CT scan, made it possible to find out much more about him, even what he ate before he died — a porridge that contained more than sixty different herbs and grasses. Scientists were also able to tell that his front tooth was knocked out when he was five, and that sickness or hunger stunted his growth when he was only three.

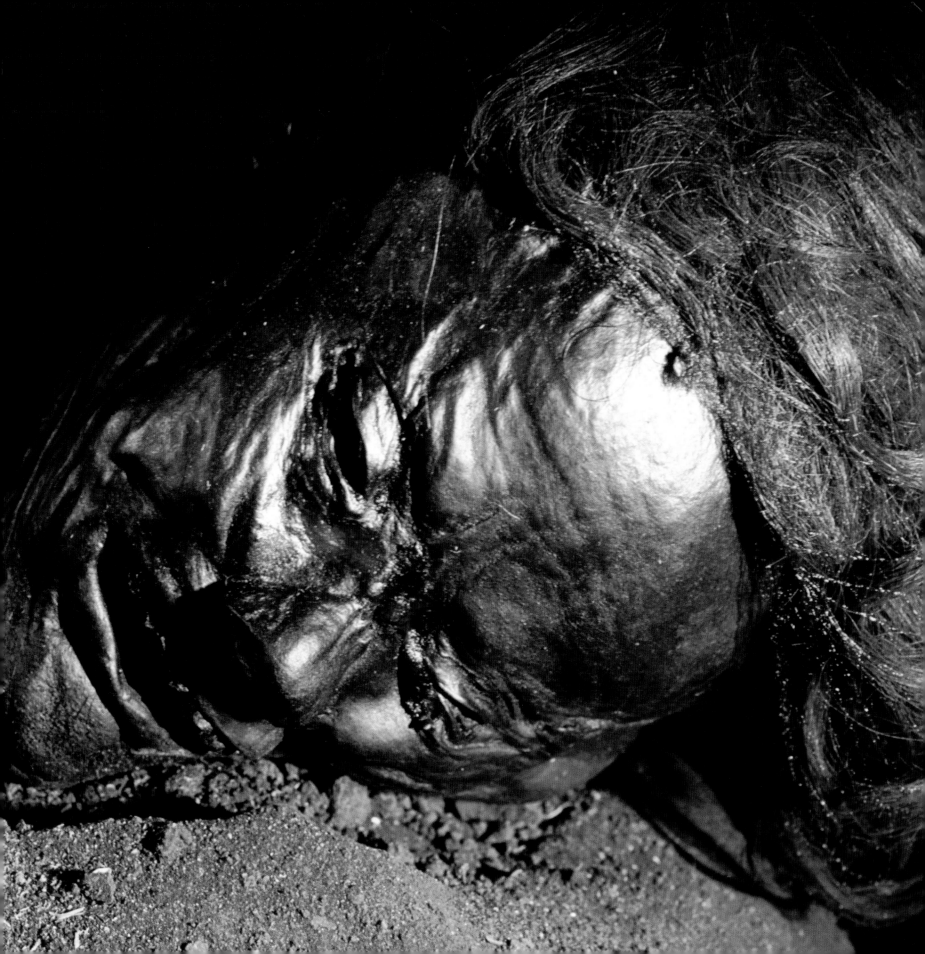

A Violent Death?

An Irish farmer was digging a drain in a peat bog near his house in 2003 when he struck something unexpected — a headless body. Clothing, skin, a bracelet on the upper arm, and even fingernails had all been preserved. Yet this person, called Croghan Hill Man after the area where he was found, likely died two thousand years ago during the Iron Age — just like Grauballe Man.

Croghan •

Almost two thousand bodies have been found in the cold, wet peat bogs of northwestern Europe. Many date back to a time when iron was first used to make tools and weapons. In those days, people lived in wooden houses in small villages, where they farmed flax and barley and tended livestock. Most of the bog people died naturally, but some have been found with slit throats, strangled necks, and stab wounds. Some were blindfolded or had their hands and feet tied. Others had been pinned into the bog with large stones or logs. A surprising number were children.

Some historians think the bogs may have been gathering places where people once worshipped gods with offerings of jewelry, pottery, weapons — and human sacrifices.

Did Croghan Hill Man die a violent death, like Grauballe Man? Did he die in the bog or was he put there later? Is his head still nearby, holding the answer to the mystery?

The oxygen-free acidic conditions in peat bogs are ideal for preserving wool fiber. This woolen suit (right) and hat (above) were recovered from bogs in Ireland.

Land of the Bog People

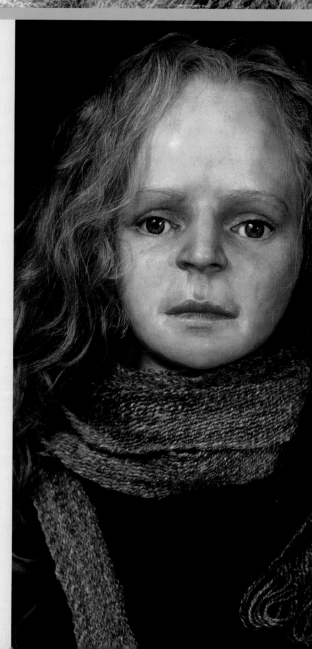

Peat bogs, like the one above, are created when plants in low-lying, watery areas die faster than they can decay. The plants pile up on top of one another, forming a dense mass of waterlogged, decaying vegetation that gradually becomes peat, which is used for fuel, among other things (peat is rich in carbon and, if left alone for a few million years, will turn into coal). There is little oxygen in the bog, so there is nothing for bacteria to feed on, and dead bodies can emerge thousands of years later, their faces shockingly lifelike.

Bogs do not affect all bodies the same way. Sometimes the skin and muscle decay. Sometimes the bones dissolve, but the skin, muscle, hair, fingernails, and eyes remain. The best preserving bogs are cold (things decay faster in the warmth) and deep (to prevent insects or animals from reaching the body). They also contain just enough tannic acid to preserve the flesh (the same way animal skin is tanned to make leather) without eating away the bones.

Yde Girl, found in a bog in the Netherlands in 1897, was sixteen when she died two thousand years ago. Recently, a medical artist reconstructed what she may have looked like before she died (right). She was only four feet, six inches tall, and X rays showed that she had an abnormally curved spine and probably walked with a limp. She had been strangled with a belt, stabbed in the throat, and her red hair had been cut off one side of her head. Was her violent death punishment for some crime?

The Mummies of Cladh Hallan

Cladh Hallan

The skeletons of a man and a woman were found in 2001 under the floor of an ancient house in Scotland (below). Their legs were drawn up under their chins, their arms wrapped around their knees.

Tests showed that the man was 3,500 years old and the woman 3,300 years old. But the same tests revealed that their bodies hadn't been buried right away. They were placed under the house hundreds of years after they had died.

Bare skeletons are not normally considered mummies. A mummy includes soft tissue that has been preserved beyond the time when it would normally have rotted away. But these skeletons were unusual. Somehow, they must have been mummified. Otherwise, during the years they had remained unburied, the skin and sinew holding the bones together would have decayed, and the skeletons would have fallen apart long before they were placed under the floor of the house.

Researchers were stunned. This was strong evidence that Europeans were intentionally making mummies around the same time as the ancient Egyptians.

How did they do it, and why? Tests showed that the bodies had been left in a peat bog for six to eighteen months — long enough to preserve the soft tissue, but not long enough to eat away more than a thin outer layer of bone.

After death, bacteria in the stomach begins to eat the bones, creating tiny holes. Scientists can find out how much bacterial activity has taken place by forcing mercury into the bones to measure the holes. Tests on

the Cladh Hallan mummies showed that bacterial growth inside these bodies had stopped shortly after death, suggesting that the stomach and intestines were removed before the bodies were placed in the bog.

No one knows why these particular bodies were deliberately preserved and buried. Maybe they belonged to village elders or priests, who were preserved and kept close to protect the village.

A Puzzling Mummy

The mummy of the man (below) was buried under the site of an ancient house (opposite) in Cladh Hallan, on the island of South Uist (above), five hundred years after he had died. But a close examination showed that the skull, jaw, and skeleton belonged to three different people! The original mummy may have been displayed before it was buried. If pieces of the body fell off, they were simply replaced with parts from other individuals.

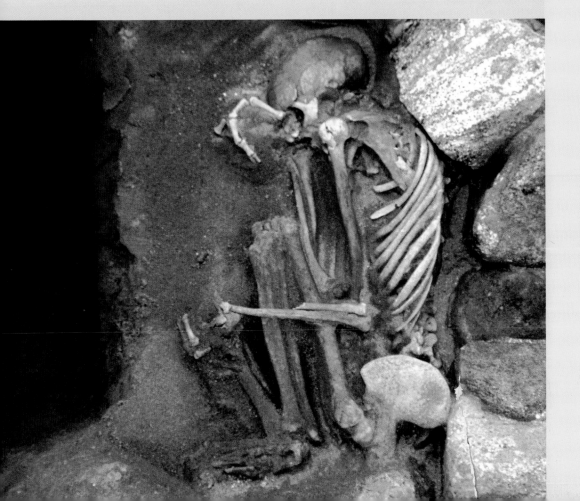

The female Cladh Hallan mummy (left) held one of her own teeth in each hand. No one knows why.

The Iceman: Mystery Solved?

Two hikers discovered the body of a man poking out of a glacier in the Ötztal Alps north of Bolzano, Italy, in 1991. When the body and the objects and clothing with it were examined, they were found to be 5,300 years old.

The news made headlines around the globe. The Iceman, the oldest complete human body ever found, is probably the best-studied mummy in the world, and new information is constantly being revealed as technology improves. The chemicals in the Iceman's teeth, for example, have been found to match those in the soil of a specific valley south of the Alps, which was probably his home. The pollen in his intestine has been identified as belonging to plants that flower in spring, meaning he was in the mountains at the end of the winter, not in the fall, as scientists first thought.

But for a long time no one knew how the Iceman had died. Did he freeze to death in his sleep, or collapse from illness or exhaustion? Why was his left arm lying across his body in such an awkward position?

The mystery may finally be solved.

Ötztal Alps

Bolzano

When the Iceman was discovered, even his eyeballs were intact — usually one of the first soft tissues to decompose after a person dies.

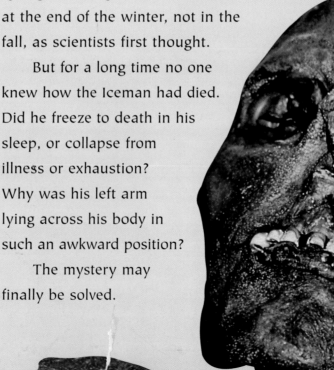

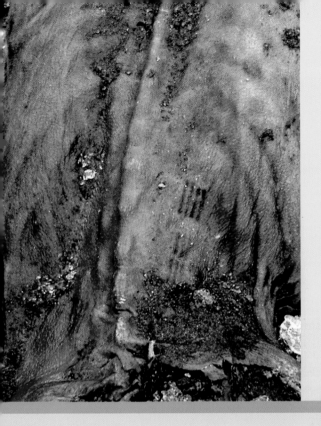

An Ancient Therapy

The Iceman had simple tattoos on his back (left), knees, ankles, and wrists (below). They had been made by inserting charcoal under the skin using a bone or wooden needle. Recently, scientists noticed that the locations of the tattoos match traditional acupuncture points used to treat back and stomach pain. Previous studies showed the Iceman suffered from both these ailments because he had arthritis of the spine and intestinal parasites.

Acupuncture is a Chinese therapy that uses small needles to treat pain. Yet the Iceman lived two thousand years before the practice is thought to have started in China.

In 2001, a CT scan revealed an arrowhead lodged in the Iceman's left shoulder. The arrow had torn through nerves and major blood vessels. DNA tests of scrapings from his knife, axe, and clothing found blood from several individuals.

Then, in 2003, researchers discovered two deep gashes on the Iceman's right hand and wrist — wounds inflicted shortly before he died.

Finally, we had a picture of the Iceman's last hours. Perhaps he strayed into the territory of an enemy tribe and was stabbed as he battled for his life. Fleeing from his attackers, he was shot in the shoulder from behind. With his left arm paralyzed and in terrible pain, he bled to death.

The Iceman's knife had a flint blade which had to be sharpened frequently. However, his bearskin hat was better suited to a cold climate than the spruce-root hat belonging to Kwaday Dan Ts'inchi (page 12).

As mummies are found around the world, people lay claim to them for different reasons. The German hikers who discovered the Iceman demanded to be paid for finding him. The Egyptian government has asked that all ancient human remains be returned to their homeland, and at the same time they have pressured archaeologists to display newly found mummies as tourist attractions.

In the Altai Mountains of Siberia, however, some local people just want a mummy put back where it was found. In 1993, a mummy called the Siberian Ice Maiden was discovered frozen in a block of ice near the border between Russia and China. Six saddled and bridled horses lay beneath the coffin. The mummy had gold earrings, a blouse made of silk that likely came from India, and a felt headdress that took up one-third of the coffin.

ASIA

(Above) The Ice Maiden's burial chamber. (Opposite) One of the horses buried with the Ice Maiden. Her people valued horses highly, both in life and in death.

Since the Ice Maiden was discovered, there has been an increase in earthquake activity in the Altai. After an earthquake in 2003 left 1,800 people homeless, some local leaders said the tremors would only stop if the Ice Maiden was reburied and her spirit allowed to rest in peace. Not surprisingly, archaeologists are opposed to giving up the mummy. Recent DNA tests have shown the 2,500-year-old mummy was of European — not Asian — origin and archaeologists want to know more about where she came from.

Other recent mummy finds in China and Siberia are also making historians reconsider what we know about how different cultures developed. Mummies may show that the links between the world's peoples are much closer than we once thought.

Medieval Graveyard

Zeleniy Yar

Archaeologists have recently unearthed bodies near the Siberian settlement of Zeleniy Yar, just south of the Arctic Circle. More than thirty graves have been opened. Most of the coffins, made of hollowed-out logs lined with birch bark, contain only shattered skeletons, but five mummies have been recovered. Four of them are little children. The fifth belongs to a red-haired man.

The mummies are about one thousand years old. They were wrapped in blankets made of reindeer, beaver, wolverine, and bear furs. Some were also covered with copper plate and masks and bound with copper bands. They had not been embalmed but were preserved naturally in the cold, dry permafrost. Bronze bowls from Persia (present-day Iran) were also found in the cemetery.

DNA tests have shown that at least one of the mummies was European. But where did they come from? Why have no bodies of adult women been identified? Why were these people living in such a harsh area, at the base of a peninsula called "end of the earth"? What groups did they trade with, and how did they get bronze bowls from a place thousands of miles away?

The adult man's face is covered with a green copper mask. His beard and hair may have turned red because of contact with bronze and copper in the grave. He had been buried in a wooden coffin with a bronze bear's-head buckle, an iron hatchet, and several arrowheads.

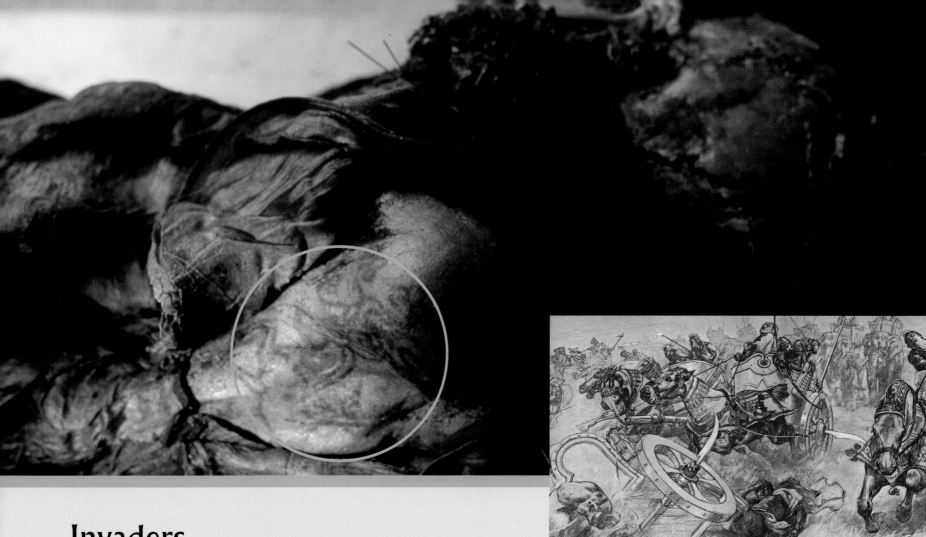

Invaders

More than two thousand years ago, a number of groups were making their way into Siberia, looking for trade and conquest. In the south, the Ice Maiden's people, part of an overall group called the Scythians, had been fanning out from the Middle East into central Asia and Ukraine.

The Scythians were nomads whose men and women were fierce warriors (middle) and legendary horse riders. The Ice Maiden even had a fantastic horse-like creature tattooed on her arm (above, circled). The Scythians were also known for their beautifully crafted weapons, clothing, and jewelry — such as this gold belt buckle (right). They wore blue tattoos of animals and mythical creatures. The Scythians often buried important individuals with their horses, saddled and sacrificed so they could accompany their masters into the afterlife. They also mummified their dead, removing the internal organs and stuffing the bodies, and taking out the brain through a large hole in the back of the skull.

31

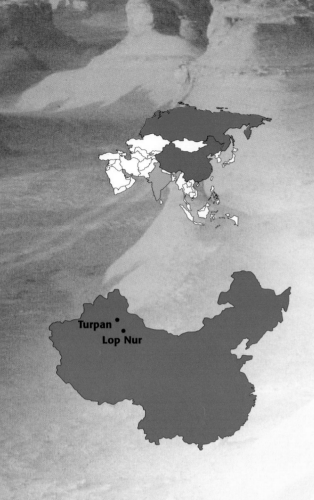

The Mummies of Xinjiang

Deep in the heart of Asia lies Xinjiang, a Chinese province that is mostly a vast desert surrounded by mountains. Two thousand years ago, Xinjiang was crossed by trade routes known as the Silk Road. Camel caravans carried ivory, gold, olive oil, salt, furs, silk, tea, and spices between Europe and China on a long, dangerous journey braving sandstorms, blizzards, and thieves.

In 2001, archaeologists found mummies poking out of a giant sand dune south of the city of Turpan. The sand dune turned out to be an ancient cemetery containing more than one hundred well-preserved bodies with their internal organs intact. The long brown hair and eyelid of a small boy could still be seen, even though the mummy was more than four thousand years old.

Well-preserved mummies that have not been embalmed offer scientists a better chance of extracting uncontaminated DNA. In the case of the Xinjiang mummies, these tests could be particularly interesting because a number of the mummies have distinct Caucasian or European features. Some of them are very tall for Asians. Some even have blond hair and pale skin.

What does this mean? Scholars have long thought that contact between China and Europe began about 2,300 years ago. But if people with European heritage were buried here more than three thousand years ago, it means Europeans and Chinese were exchanging goods and knowledge much, much earlier.

Could the Iceman's people have had contact with people from China five thousand years ago? Further tests may provide the answer.

More than one hundred mummies have been discovered buried in a sand dune in a desolate place known as Lop Nur (background), near the city of Turpan, China. The extremely dry environment has helped to preserve the bodies naturally over many centuries.

Hot, Salty, and Dry: A Recipe for Making Mummies

Cherchen Man was almost six feet tall, with pale skin, light brown hair, and a long nose. He was buried in Xinjiang around 1000 BCE, long before Europeans were thought to have first visited China. A dead horse and saddle had been placed on top of his grave.

Did ancient travelers make their way across the continent on horseback thousands of years ago?

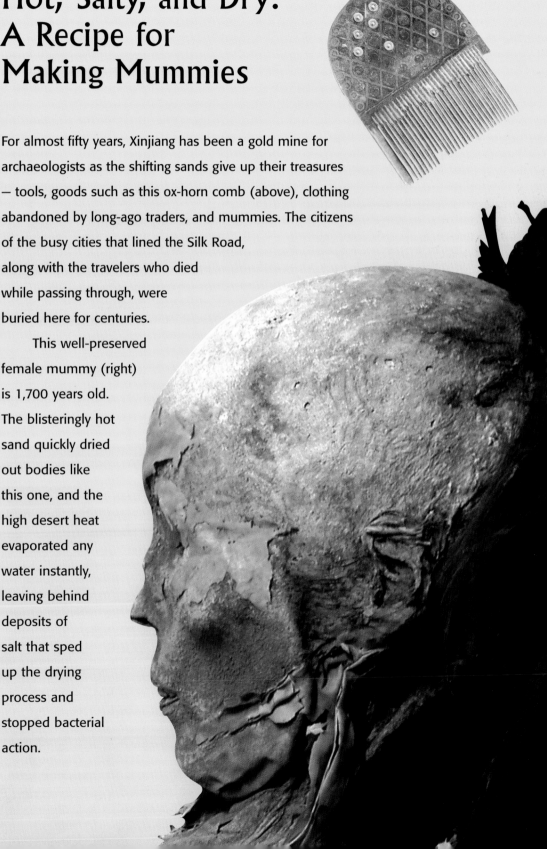

For almost fifty years, Xinjiang has been a gold mine for archaeologists as the shifting sands give up their treasures — tools, goods such as this ox-horn comb (above), clothing abandoned by long-ago traders, and mummies. The citizens of the busy cities that lined the Silk Road, along with the travelers who died while passing through, were buried here for centuries.

This well-preserved female mummy (right) is 1,700 years old. The blisteringly hot sand quickly dried out bodies like this one, and the high desert heat evaporated any water instantly, leaving behind deposits of salt that sped up the drying process and stopped bacterial action.

Becoming a Mummy

Many cultures have preserved their dead as part of their religious beliefs. In some remote monasteries in Asia, however, there are monks who have preserved their bodies by trying to turn themselves into mummies *before* death.

In 2003, scientists confirmed that the mummy of a Buddhist monk, Sangha Tenzin, had been found near the tiny village of Ghuen in India's Himalayas. Carbon dating showed that the mummy was more than five hundred years old, yet even the eyeballs were intact. The internal organs had not been removed, and the body had not been treated with chemicals in any way. Experts said the man had, in effect, mummified himself.

Self-mummification has been practiced by monks in Asia for hundreds of years. Different techniques were practiced in different regions, but the basic stages were the same. The monk would first go on a strict diet, eating no rice, barley, or beans. Instead he would eat certain seeds, nuts, bark, roots, and perhaps drink a special tea made

• Ghuen

The mummies of monks have been found in the Himalayan mountains (below), where the extremely cold, dry air has helped to preserve them.

from tree sap. The tea would cause dehydration but was also toxic, preventing insects and bacteria from attacking the body after death.

At the same time, the monk would meditate and slow down his breathing. He would not move and he would eventually stop eating (one monk was said to be able to meditate for up to fifteen days without food or water). His muscles would relax, reducing their need for oxygen. His heart rate and blood pressure would lower. Some monks sat surrounded by candles to dry out their bodies even more.

In time, the internal organs could shrink to one-quarter their normal size from lack of use. By the time the monk finally stopped breathing, his body was not much more than skin and bones, with little soft tissue to feed decay. If the body could then be completely dried before decay took over, it became a mummy.

In spite of these efforts, the natural process of decay could often not be stopped, and most bodies rotted anyway. The successful mummies are sometimes displayed as inspiration for their followers.

The mummy of Buddhist monk Luang Pho Daeng, who died in 1973, sits in a shrine in Thailand. Sunglasses hide his shriveled eye sockets.

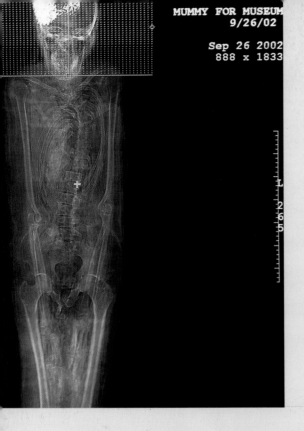

MUMMY FOR MUSEUM
9/26/02

Sep 26 2002
888 x 1833

In the past, people made mummies so bodies could be reunited with their spirits in the afterlife. Others made mummies to remember their loved ones, just as we might display photographs of our relatives today.

People still preserve the dead for many of the same reasons. Sometimes political and religious leaders are mummified to inspire their followers. Mummies are also made to teach future doctors about anatomy, or to display as art.

Today, many people are temporarily preserved after death. Modern embalming began in the 1860s during the American Civil War to preserve soldiers' bodies until they could be sent back to their families for burial.

Modern embalming is really not that different from ancient Egyptian mummification. In a funeral home, a mortician replaces the body fluids

MODERN MUMMIES

Modern technologies have created new ways of looking at mummies. Diagnostic tools like CT scans — such as this 2002 scan of an unidentified mummy in Boston (above) — can provide detailed information about a person's diet, age, and gender. And a recent technique called plastination (opposite) gives three-dimensional views of the blood vessels, bones, and muscles of real human bodies.

with chemicals, uses makeup and padding to make the body appear lifelike, and dresses the body so it can be displayed before being buried or cremated. Yet embalming only postpones the process of decay.

What should be done with the dead? It takes several gallons of oil to cremate a body. An embalmed body in a coffin can take decades to decompose, and embalming chemicals can seep into groundwater. In Britain, some people are choosing to be buried simply in a biodegradable coffin with a tree planted on top, in cemeteries that look more like parks than graveyards.

As the world's population grows beyond six billion, dealing with the dead is not a simple issue. How can we best honor the dead? Thousands of years ago, ancient peoples were asking themselves that same question.

Famous Mummies

Displaying dead political and religious leaders helps keep their memories alive and inspires their followers.

Eva Peron (right), the wife of Argentine president Juan Peron, was hugely popular, particularly among the poor. She was also a famous figure worldwide (bottom, left). After she died in 1952, lines of mourners six deep stretched for thirty blocks in different directions, and many people waited for sixteen hours to pay their respects. Her body was mummified using wax and acetate.

When Juan Peron was overthrown in 1955, the new government was afraid Eva Peron's body might inspire the poor to revolution, so they buried it secretly in Italy. The body was eventually returned, and it now lies under several layers of steel in a tomb in Buenos Aires (bottom right).

Russian revolutionary Vladimir Ilyich Lenin died in 1924. He had wished to be buried beside his mother, but his body (right) was considered too important a symbol for Communist Russia. Instead, it was embalmed in stages similar to those used by the ancient Egyptians. First the brain and internal organs were removed and the body was dried. Then the skin was softened in a glycerin bath. Finally, it was encased in a waterproof suit before being dressed.

The Russian leader has been on public display in Moscow ever since. However, even with constant maintenance by a team of fifteen scientists, the body continues to decay. Every year and a half it must be soaked in a moisturizing solution for a month. The hands and head are bathed in embalming fluid twice a week.

Mao Zedong, founder of the People's Republic of China, is still a hero to millions of Chinese, even though he died in 1976. Mao had wanted to be cremated, but officials decided to have his body (left) permanently preserved. His internal organs are kept in jars like those of the ancient Egyptian kings. Every year, more than five million visitors file past his crystal casket in Tiananmen Square.

Mummy Art

In 2004, an exhibition opened at the California Science Center in Los Angeles. It was called *Body Worlds: The Anatomical Exhibition of Real Human Bodies*. The exhibits were modern mummies — human bodies that had been preserved through plastination, a process that replaces the fat and water in cells with clear plastic.

These kinds of mummies are not new. In the 1700s, a French anatomist named Honoré Fragonard made mummies by stripping the bodies of skin, injecting them with colored wax, soaking them in alcohol, and drying them. The mummified bodies were used as teaching tools in anatomy schools.

Can mummies be art? Some historians say the Chinchorro mummies are as much sculptures as preserved bodies. Tutankhamun's gold mummy mask is often considered to be the most beautiful object ever found anywhere, and the painted caskets of later Egyptian mummies are thought to be some of the finest portraits in art history.

What makes mummies art? Compare the Chinchorro mummy (above, left) to a carving from the same period. (Right) A beautiful gilded mummy case from the Bahariya Oasis.

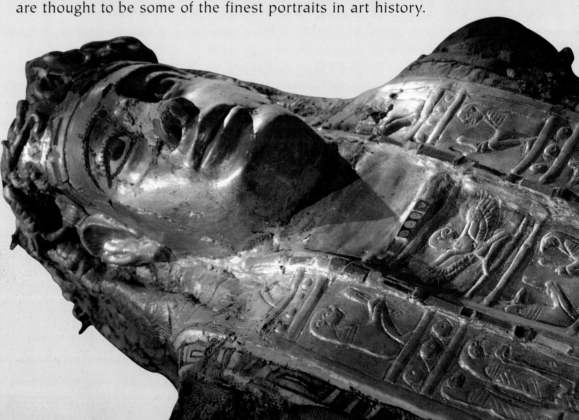

40

Dead animal bodies are also preserved as art. Hunters may take their kill to a taxidermist, who peels off the skin, preserves it, and stuffs it, perhaps adding glass eyes or a wax nose to make the body look lifelike. The animal is then mounted on a wall or in a glass case to be admired as a trophy.

Mummies have been bought, sold, collected, and displayed by individuals and museums ever since they were first found — for the simple reason that people want to look at them. The exhibition of plastinated mummies has toured around the world, drawing more than seventeen million visitors.

Fragonard created *The Horseman of the Apocalypse* using the bodies of a real man and horse (right) between 1766 and 1771. (Left) Schoolchildren examine a plastinated body at an exhibition in Tokyo.

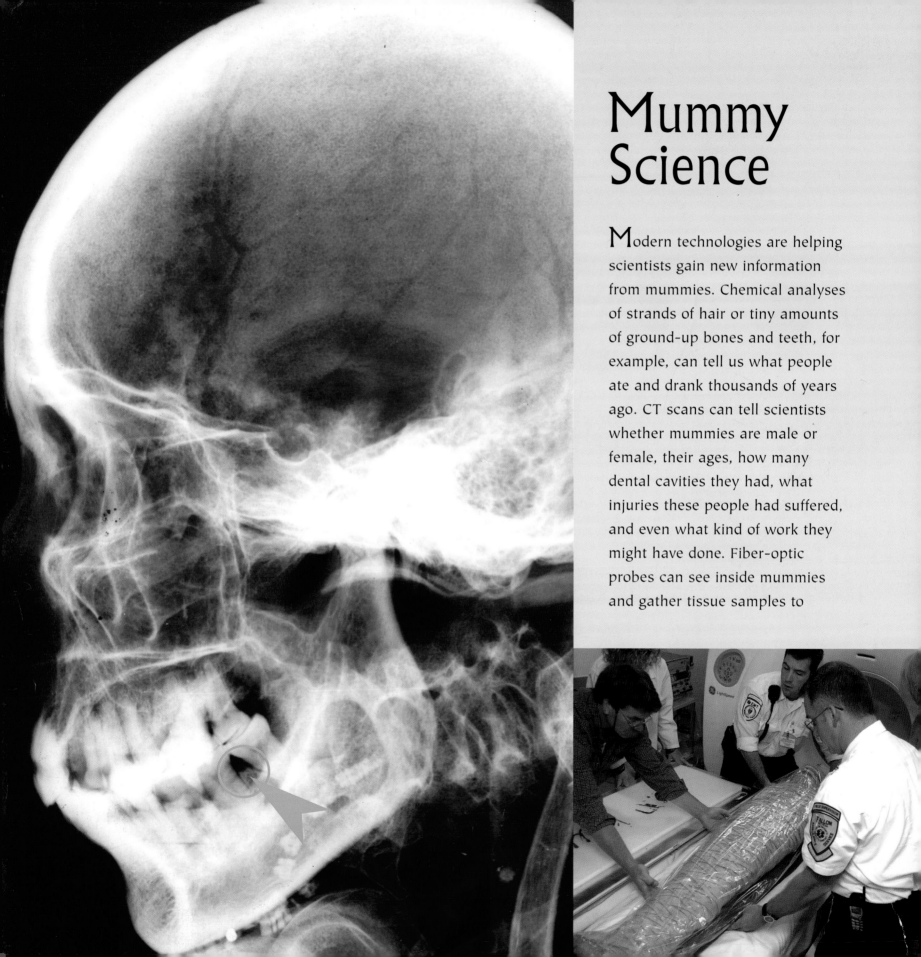

Mummy Science

Modern technologies are helping scientists gain new information from mummies. Chemical analyses of strands of hair or tiny amounts of ground-up bones and teeth, for example, can tell us what people ate and drank thousands of years ago. CT scans can tell scientists whether mummies are male or female, their ages, how many dental cavities they had, what injuries these people had suffered, and even what kind of work they might have done. Fiber-optic probes can see inside mummies and gather tissue samples to determine what diseases a person had and what medicines or herbs were used to treat them. Tests for DNA, the genetic blueprint that is different for each individual, can reveal who was related to whom, and may even help us trace the origins of inherited diseases.

All these tests reveal that people of the past had many of the same diseases we have (though they seldom suffered from heart disease or cancer). They had gum disease and dental cavities and were crippled with arthritis. Ancient people in Egypt and the Americas had tuberculosis. And people everywhere suffered and died from intestinal parasites and malaria, as millions still do today.

X rays and CT scans can provide detailed information about mummies while allowing the bodies to remain in their wrappings. An X ray of an Inca mummy (opposite, left) shows the bone pulling away from the teeth (circled), a sign of gum disease. A CT scan of the Boston mummy in 2002 (opposite, right) showed that the body was male. Evidence of decomposition revealed he had not been mummified immediately after death.

Freezing for Eternity

Cryonics (from the Greek word for cold) involves cooling bodies immediately after death until almost all decay stops. The body is then stored in liquid nitrogen, in the hope that medical advances will one day be able to cure the disease that caused the person to die in the first place. At that point the body could perhaps be thawed and "reanimated," or brought back to life.

Extreme cold does preserve organisms. Meat can be kept in a freezer for a long time before rotting. Ice tombs have preserved mummies for thousands of years. Even today, the human heart can be kept on ice for eight hours and transplanted into another person. And on rare occasions, drowning victims have been revived after they have been in freezing water for as long as an hour.

But when ice crystals form, they tear cells apart. That's why frostbitten toes and fingers turn black. As soon as the blood stops bringing all-important oxygen, cell damage begins to occur — so no one knows exactly how "animated" a defrosted body would actually be.

In *Star Wars: The Empire Strikes Back*, Han Solo (below) is "frozen" in carbonite and then brought back to life. But for now, bringing the frozen back to life is still more fiction than science.

In 2001, two years after the Canadian mummy Kwaday Dan Ts'inchi was discovered, he was given to the area's native people and cremated in a closed ceremony. The ashes were scattered over the glacier where he had been found. No photographs of the mummy were ever published, although scientists continue to study tissue samples from the body.

At the recently discovered ancient cemetery at Bahariya, Egypt, tombs are deliberately being left unexplored to disturb as few graves as possible. The head of the excavation says he is torn between wanting to know what the mummies can tell us about their world, and not wanting to intrude upon the dead. Should mummies be left alone when we have the tools to learn so much from them?

Children play at the edge of an Inca cemetery being excavated in their schoolyard in Tupac Amaru, Peru. Archaeologists can only hope they reach other historic sites like this before they are bulldozed to make way for modern development.

EPILOGUE

Today, more than 150 scientists from around the world are studying the Iceman and finding out more about the world he lived in. The mummy and his tools, weapons, and belongings continue to reveal new information about ancient European clothing, medicine, farming, diseases, and diet. They will keep scientists busy for generations to come.

The Iceman now resides in a refrigerated cell in the South Tyrol Museum of Archaeology in Bolzano, Italy.

As for the Iceman himself, he is housed in his own museum in Bolzano, Italy. Located at the entrance is a gift shop where you can buy Iceman T-shirts, puzzles, postcards, and refrigerator magnets. On the second floor are the exhibits that describe his life and display his possessions — his grass cloak, his dagger, his copper axe, and his longbow and flint-tipped arrows.

Finally, at the top of a short ramp, there is a little square window. Through the window you can see the Iceman lying on a glass table in an ice-lined room. He looks small. Even though he has been kept carefully frozen under the strictest conditions, the Iceman is half the size he was when he was found. Ever since he has been out of the frozen tomb where he was perfectly preserved for 5,300 years, he continues to shrink a bit each day.

Visitors become very quiet and thoughtful when they see the Iceman. While mummies draw us first with the sight of their wasted, blackened bodies and their crumbling, slack faces, there's more to our fascination than that. Mummies are windows to ancient people who often left behind no record besides a few of their belongings and their own bodies. Scientists now have the tools to read those bodies and find out a great deal about the world they lived in thousands of years ago.

TIMELINE*

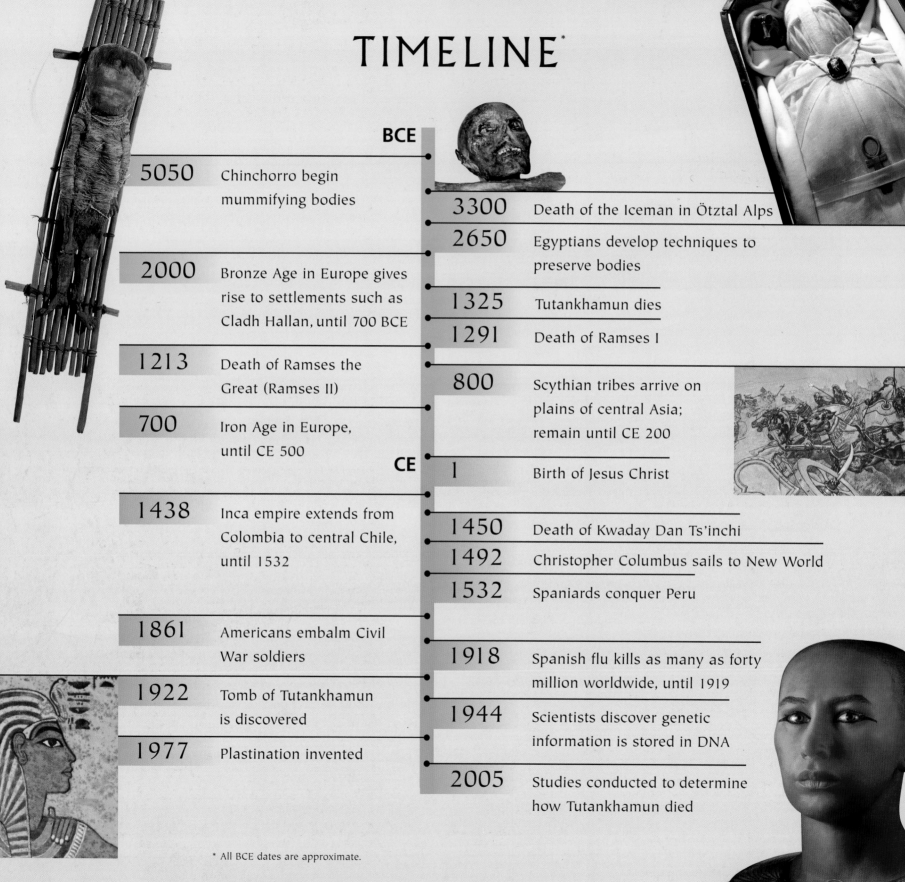

BCE

5050	Chinchorro begin mummifying bodies
3300	Death of the Iceman in Ötztal Alps
2650	Egyptians develop techniques to preserve bodies
2000	Bronze Age in Europe gives rise to settlements such as Cladh Hallan, until 700 BCE
1325	Tutankhamun dies
1291	Death of Ramses I
1213	Death of Ramses the Great (Ramses II)
800	Scythian tribes arrive on plains of central Asia; remain until CE 200
700	Iron Age in Europe, until CE 500

CE

1	Birth of Jesus Christ
1438	Inca empire extends from Colombia to central Chile, until 1532
1450	Death of Kwaday Dan Ts'inchi
1492	Christopher Columbus sails to New World
1532	Spaniards conquer Peru
1861	Americans embalm Civil War soldiers
1918	Spanish flu kills as many as forty million worldwide, until 1919
1922	Tomb of Tutankhamun is discovered
1944	Scientists discover genetic information is stored in DNA
1977	Plastination invented
2005	Studies conducted to determine how Tutankhamun died

* All BCE dates are approximate.

GLOSSARY

acetate: a form of acid that is often used to create plastics

amulet: a piece of jewelry

archaeologist: someone who studies people from the past as well as their cultures

arthritis: a painful swelling of the joints in the body

BCE: Before the Common Era, the years before the birth of Jesus Christ

biodegradable: capable of decomposing with the help of microorganisms

Caucasian: descended from native Europeans, North Africans, West Asians, or Indians, or from language groups in the region of the Caucasus mountains in southeastern Europe

CE: Common Era, the years after the birth of Jesus Christ

Communism: a system of government controlled by one political party that runs the state-owned means of production

DNA: deoxyribonucleic acid, a complex chemical compound found in cells that carries hereditary information

epidemic: a widespread occurrence of a disease

fiber-optics: a technology that allows information to travel by light signals through glass fibers

glacier: a large, slow-moving mass of ice

glycerin: a thick liquid that is created when fats turn into soap

natron: a naturally occurring form of salt found in dry lake beds

nomad: a member of a group of people who travel from place to place in search of food or pasture

permafrost: a permanently frozen layer of soil

radiocarbon dating: a method to determine age by measuring how much carbon-14 it contains

resin: a solid or semisolid substance that comes from plants

shantytown: a poor area of a town consisting of roughly built homes

spondylus: a thorny oyster whose shell was considered valuable, particularly by the ancient peoples of the Andes

tannic acid: a chemical that is used in many industries, from leather making to wine making

tuberculosis: an infectious disease that produces small bumps, especially on the lungs, creating difficulty breathing

virus: a microscopic organism that uses a host cell to multiply, and usually carries a disease

SELECTED BIBLIOGRAPHY

Arriaza, Bernardo. "Chinchorro Mummies." *National Geographic*, March 1995, 68-89.

Cock, Guillermo A. "Inca Rescue." *National Geographic*, May 2002, 78-91.

Keys, David. "The Mummies of Cladh Hallan." The BBC online, http://www.bbc.co.uk/history/archaeology/mummies_cladh hallan_01.shtml.

Marston, Wendy. "Making a Modern Mummy." *Discover*, March 2000, 70-75.

RECOMMENDED READING

For readers ages eight to twelve:

A Gift for Ampato by Susan Vande Griek (Groundwood). Based on the discovery of Juanita, a child mummy found in Peru in 1995, this novel tells the story of her last days.

Mummies by John Malam (Kingfisher). An overview of mummies from different cultures and countries. Includes resources.

Mummies, Bones, and Body Parts by Charlotte Wilcox (Carolrhoda Books). A look at how human remains are found and analyzed to uncover their scientific and historical significance.

For older readers:

The Mummies of Ürümchi by Elizabeth Wayland Barber (Norton). An in-depth study of Tarim Basin mummies and artifacts.

Written in Bones, consultant editor Paul Bahn (Firefly Books). Case studies of archaeological sites around the world.

PICTURE CREDITS

INDEX

ACKNOWLEDGMENTS

The author and Madison Press Books would like to thank Paul Bahn for lending his considerable expertise to this project; Gerald Conlogue, director of diagnostic imaging at Quinnipiac University in Connecticut and co-host of *The Mummy Roadshow*, for generously supplying images and information; Michael Parker Pearson at the University of Sheffield for kindly allowing us to use his images; William Fitzhugh and Helena Sharp from the Smithsonian National Museum of Natural History Arctic Studies Center for providing invaluable photos and knowledge; Sheila Greer at Champagne and Aishihik First Nations, Canadian Heritage, Special Projects, for going to great lengths to supply us with images; Victor Mair, professor of Chinese language and literature at the University of Pennsylvania, for his generous consultation; and Najla Semple for her assistance with gathering information.

ISBN-10: 1-895892-89-9
ISBN-13: 978-1-895892-89-5

12 11 10 9 8 7 6 5 4 3 2 1   6 7 8 9 10 11/0

Printed in China by Lotus Printing

First Scholastic printing, 2006

MUMMIES: THE NEWEST, COOLEST & CREEPIEST FROM AROUND THE WORLD
was produced by

MADISON PRESS BOOKS
1000 Yonge Street, Suite 200
Toronto, Ontario, Canada
M4W 2K2
www.madisonpressbooks.com

Project Editors: Shima Aoki, Imoinda Romain
Editorial Director: Wanda Nowakowska

Designer: Diana Sullada
Art Director: Jennifer Lum

Production Manager: Sandra L. Hall
Production Director: Susan Barrable

Publisher: Oliver Salzmann